AF323764

Beasts

Miriam Sagan

© 2020 Miriam Sagan
Cover photograph and design © 2020 Susan Gardner
© Author's photograph by Matt Morrow, 2019

All rights reserved. No part of this book may be reproduced in any form, by any means, electronic or mechanical, without permission in writing from the author, except for brief quotations for the purpose of reviews.

Many of these poems were written during two artist-in-residence stints with the National Park Service, at Hot Springs National Park in Arkansas and at Agate Fossil Beds National Monument in Nebraska. Many thanks to the program, administrators, and rangers for the opportunity to live and write in these unique settings.

"Beasts in the Earth" and other poems were written during a "Microscopic" residency at Ayatana/Art Loves Science in Ontario, Canada.

Some of these poems first appeared in the following magazines and e-zines:
Ayatana Botanical Anthology—Germinating Herbarium, Free Lit, Independent Variable, Inlandia, Poetic Diversity, Thimble, Taos Review, Versewrights, What Rough Beast

978-1-7326501-6-9
Printed in the United States of America

RED MOUNTAIN PRESS
www.redmountainpress.us

PAPER LANTERN MOSS

beneath the dissecting microscope—
coastline of a lost world
fog, regret, the little plane
seeming to fall
out of the sky,
the smell of saltwater.

When I saw
my childhood friends
at the funeral
my feet remembered
every twist and root and cool patch
of sand
on the path
through cranberries
to the beach,
route I'd retrace
in winter nights
before sleep
far from those dunes.

Really, those were the details
of being in love,
my first confusion
between people and place,
the love that was a kind of
completion,
of arrival.

WHAT IS LOCKED

1.
hidden springs grotto
with its iron grille and bolt

I Love Jesus
scratched in stone by the bench

nervous graffiti
in the nether regions of mother earth

2.
world of sleep
sealed off from morning coffee

recurring dream
of a sad city

ruined
basilica

3.
the heart

4.
mountainside
with its flight
of stone steps

I'm too crippled
to walk up
mountain laurel

5.
green earth forgotten
like a rusted key

and no one
remembers
the doors it opens

THE FOREST HAS EARS, THE FIELD HAS EYES

in the dark of the gorge
music—brief—intermittent

as the hardwood forest
plays itself

open
like a grand piano

in the sketch by Hieronymous Bosch
an enormous owl

and literal
eyeballs scattered on the grass

ears on the trunk
pine, oak, hickory, maple

gum seed balls
crunching underfoot

I saw the gulch, the woods
and it all saw me

neither
kind nor indifferent

just a puttering neighbor
doing its own thing

the stream rushes away
cold with fish

in the tunnel it meets
water hot from the earth

pure, inhospitable
to catfish, crawdaddies

darkness
embraces all I have to give

my words, a snatch of a song
sung over and over

arms, lips
I kissed the house

good-bye
in a tender spot

over the front door
light switch

and was gone
myself.

Battle of Punished Woman's Fork, Kansas, 1878

I ask the lady at the desk
at the state park
what the name means

she says—in eleven years here
no one has asked that question—
but she doesn't offer any answer

the land
is covered in marks
so too the map

although the soil itself
might just crumble
through our fingers

nothing to tell me
who is Punished Woman
and what was her fate

but is there any
portion of earth
that might not

bear
her name?

INDIAN PIPES

pale fungus in pine forest
silent
plays no
music, nothing
to draw the ear
from the usual
beach house
family quarrels.

I have heard
forests play themselves,
crystal woods
reverberate
like gamelans,
but never on that island
so dominated
on every side
by the sound
of the sea.

Palm Reader

I see you hesitate
at the mouth
of the alley
of red blossoms and
drug dealers.

Also, wonder
if you need
two for the price
of one
rhinestone sandals.

Believe me:
you don't.

You can't have
one thing without the other,
your lifeline
shows death
just by ending.

Enjoy
this state of mind.

The past is gone
(you heard that here first, and
for a price.)
Go on
into your future
that must resemble it.

I suggest sneakers
as your shoes
for feet that hurt.
Your fate is you.

There's money in your palm
so don't
go barefoot.

Water Gods

The feminine offering—
an Indian maiden
proffers a bowl of water
to conquistador de Soto
who may—or may not—
have passed this way.
A sentimental statue
on the segregated
men's side
of the grand bath house.
Made up Indian names
and made up
Indian myths—
even the conquerors
feel the unease of the conquered land itself.

Rain gods sit on a shelf—
Pottery made by the great
Nampeyo of Hopi—
They're real
in that they're
shaped by her hand,
painted in colors
of the desert,
and fake in that
they have nothing to do
with Arkansas, or these
pure springs
that gush
from the earth
in a place that never
lacks for rain.

The black attendant
and the white woman in the bath—
Sarah cast Hagar
into the wilderness
bondswoman and child
to starve
but ravens fed them
as if they were prophets.
God of the waters
and of the dry wadi
we're looking to
fall into you
even from this
great distance.

At the Intersection

of Chemin de Solitude North
and Solitude East
ditches full of flowers
gone to seed
as have I,
although not too
creaky this morning,
walking in autumn
unfamiliar, yet
reminiscent.

PRAIRIE LIKE A BRIDE

clouds, dunes of ash
    sand, grit
drifted with an ageless wind
from ancient volcanoes
fossil soil

in drought
it's flesh
that comes to water
departs as bone
twenty million years old

badlands that eroded out
of the past
that we are trying to read
like a WPA mural
on a county building
or a winter count
painted on hide
that begins
with the creation
of the world

skeleton of a tipi
sunflowers gone to seed
a field of supernovas
yellow butterfly
among September's
dry clanking stalks

cushion
gray velveteen
stuck with pins
wild cucumber
twining the bridge

weed called needle and thread
stinging nettles

a ribbon
marked the place
where I'd stopped reading
interrupted
by a child
wanting a glass of water

blank pages
of this book
ruffled by breeze
hair in my mouth
as if everything
were speaking to me
at once

a woman's life is…
wind wind wind
the mind of God
is moving again

and I with it.

THE PRAIRIE ERASES THE SELF

or hangs it
on a hook

a worn dress
faded print

of pink madras
or sprigged blue

with the pockets
pulled shapeless

by the weight
of agate pebbles

gathered from a stream
the weight

of scanning
360 degrees of horizon

of being the center
of ever widening circles.

The Devil's Corkscrew

tiny horses
    whose hooves
    still beat
    a tattoo
    on earth's submission

a wort
whose classical name
means
cold goddess of the moon

daemonelix—
a fossil
Victorian gentlemen
in collars
thought was the root
of an enormous tree

rather it is the burrow
of prehistoric
beavers

the paleontologist
must pretend
to understand time

even
when thoughts
come round again

of the invisible
your predecessor's handwriting
labels
the type specimens
in a safe.

Diatoms
who live in glass houses
shouldn't…

If you are an alga
the most crucial
thing in your life
is to stay up
towards sunlight,

at least right now
in the morphology
of the interim.

RED CLOUD

1.

lace curtains
Venus at dusk
Nebraska

an old story—
wind ruffles
the pages of a book

no longer salvage—
an expensive quilt;
prairie, wind, train whistle

loneliness
made more lonely
by a lonely tale

2.

blue horses
come over the ridge
of the mind

warriors painted on hide

songlines tell us about
    water/no water

even a small girl
in her nightgown
might fly barefoot
over the town's steeples
and train tracks

every thing
in its essence
yearns
to go elsewhere

Back to School

milkweed pods empty
it's autumn

on the field trip
the only purple haired girl

holds her sister with Down syndrome
on her lap, already

an expression of worn love and care
etched on her childish face

three little girls walk
as one across a national park parking lot

the one in the middle—
lightest? most loved?

squashed by the other two
no one will let go

almost everyone says
they dream of flying

just one boy says
he wishes he could see Jesus

weather is either bad or good
according to the teacher

and rain?
it's good for cows

wind? it's good for windmills
which is good for cows

climb a ladder to the sky
write a postcard to a cloud

wish
you were here

watching the kids circle
buzz, rearrange, and toss

like molecules
at the start of time

where life began
trying to be us.

Even the Pathogen

yearns to live

and flourish.
There's a black squirrel

at the bird feeder.
You might prefer

chickadees, but
contrary

to expectation
these woods

are not ours.

Winter Count

you can start
the story
from the center
spiral out

horses rush
across painted hide
of this year's war
the power
of just
touching the enemy
with a finger

I'm a girl
I don't know
how to start
with this
I'm not that girl, still
oh yes
I am

I'm not going to tell you
every terrifying thing
that ever
happened to me

my maternal grandmother
sees the child
next to her trampled to death
by horsemen

what shall we do?
get on a boat
head west
to Ellis Island

horses again
out of Central Asia
red or green
not the blue ones
of dreams

I never drank
anything left opened
at a party
I never left
any woman I knew
behind
drunk or asleep

I didn't wear
a bra
in New York City
and got chased
down a side street
I gave the finger
and ran
really fast

I'm still running
breathless

I promised myself
I'd say
no more than this

I just took a Greyhound bus
west

massacre to massacre
star to star
invisible lines
imaginary borders

what is possessed
what can't be owned
drawn
on this body
of earth.

BEASTS IN THE EARTH

that eat decay,
autumnal forest,
the rotting log,
devour the death
of others.

Slug or snail
slimed
the pure white cup
of fungal fruit.

You also
took a bite
went down
time's wormhole.

You thought it was
a brilliant red
eyelash mushroom
instead
an M & M
someone had dropped—
by mistake?
or like breadcrumbs
to mark
a path.

In every drop
of stream water
paramecium or hydra
hunting,
predator

of a tiny world
invisible to my eye.

That's why
I had to explain
by comparison
to the visible.

BOTANICA

no one here
likes thistle
roadside or field
everyone
tries to kill it
with mowing, or
hostile insects

it's not from here
it's from Canada
or Kansas, or Texas
or Russia, or someplace worse…
and cows can't eat it

meanwhile
all the buffalo have been shot
from the train

and rhizomes beneath the surface
spread as noxious weed

it's beautiful
sturdy flower
turning to down
named milkvetch, mountain cat's eye,
narrow leaf, beardtongue

some plants are good
for what ails women
some are not—
death camas, witch grass, devil's beggartick,
rush skeleton plant

each has its secret
and persistent life
beyond ours.

The Watershed

seen from the air—
each marbled piece
seems a map
of the heat of the earth,
green twists
show the forest trail
and me
crossing the stepping stones
to a path
marked by a pink splash

it isn't that some
New York abstract expressionist
has splattered these hardwoods
rather, a pioneering
doctor in the last century
created hikes
whose steepness
rehabilitates the heart
with red
for the most difficult

so why do I dream
that you've left me
or that
I've sold the house
by mistake
or lost a job
I've already quit?
looking down
on the sumi prints
I pulled
late at night
seeing how water
carries color

how form
is fractal
unfolding
in a baking pan
I use to cook
these pink orange black
swirls
I wish I could see
ceaseless flow,
call it—my life.

EVERY MORNING

on the same walk—
the man on motorbike
(who now waves)
the irate poodle
cold student
waiting for the bus
back to the street.

One more year has passed.

Cocoons of moths
hang still
in the suburban house.

The physicist
removed
one color
from the seven
of the rainbow
and lit paper on fire
with a blue laser.

Cities fall
but I have not yet
caught the exact moment
when the suspension bridges
of my childhood
collapse into empty space.

MINUTEMAN

an aquifer named for a lost language
no espresso
too much wind

Minuteman Missile
national park site—
Canticle for Leibowitz
in the bookstore
"It's the superintendent's
favorite book"
and one of mine

and we've survived
long enough
to collect
our social security
and hold hands
out on these plains
despite everything

Bath Attendant: Nymph of The Glade

Here's a dry towel,
no—you need
to keep those
flipflops on!
(Ugly, yes, and $20.00
but you
didn't plan ahead.)
Now drink
this cup of water,
the problem with most people
is they're dehydrated
and don't know it.
Have you heard of
arnica? It's good
for aches and pains,
we all need it.
The chairs are taken.
Did you shower first?
Leaving so soon?
Honey, even if you're
stark naked
in the locker room
I'll have an opinion
on what you're wearing.
And when you walk quietly
past me
beneath the magnolias
smoking my cigarette
on my federally mandated OSHA break
I'll enjoin you, sweetheart,
to have the nicest of days
and come back.

I wasn't always
just a skinny old lady—
you see my statue
outside the once grand,
still towering, hotel—
the lovely spirit of the springs
voluptuous and unclothed
surrounded by the creatures of the glen
a stag, a doe, a fawn, a human child—
nothing
can live without me,
I embrace all
and although my shapely legs
say I can walk on earth
water is my element
where I can swim.

Outside of Town

mammoths
lie in the earth.

The check-out lady
has a story
she tells herself

as do I.
The mammoths
are in my story

but not in hers.
It's useless
to compare kinds of suffering

and it isn't kind.
There are so many bones
lifted in whirlwind.

These beasts
will never
walk the earth again

which is currently
called
South Dakota.

studying nematodes
says, "every day"
I see the hand of God.

I've seen them
making love
(he doesn't say
"mate" or "copulate.")

He says
they are like the knife
of a Mongolian host
in a yurt
cutting meat.

Says, "each day
I love them more,
and have to
kill them."

AFTER MARI SANDOZ, 1896-1966

her father beats her,
she becomes a writer,
along the upper Niobrara

Crazy Woman Creek,
a place called
Hanging Woman,
"the coming of barbed wire
the walking plow
a curl of smoke
coffee boiling at sundown"

everything
in the universe is round—
sun, moon,
time
except for stone

try this in the first person

A Herd of Buffalo

forceful dark forms
cross the highway—tourists
snap
photographs
from their automobiles

the relationship
between these things
is obscure
like a stick of charcoal
in the beautiful
art student's hand
or the mountains of the full moon
or an eclipse
of dreams

things seem to be closer to me
in the dark
more "real" as if it were this world of forms
seen flickering
by firelight
on the wall of the cave

bison shadow—
there's a girl in petticoats
dancing in a field
no, that comes later

the beasts are shaggy, shaped
and massive, horned
each mother with a calf—
to see them
is to think of what
hunger does
to all of us

ZOLTAR

Zoltar sees all
head and torso in a glass box

mechanical fortune teller
in the arcade, far from deluxe,

on the penny side of the street
by the crystal shop and museum of waxworks.

Stentorian voice of fate or doom
he sees the poet's key is in the lock

who has travelled far
to get this luck to work

like ladies on the promenade
who live in hope

for husbands and sons-in-law
and in the mineral waters seek

reducing diet or
the youthful chance for health.

The flapper's dress swings fringe
the gangster smiles at beauty with his wealth

worn out by Jim Crow slavery
the free are marching in the street

a boy grows up, believes—he knows—
he will be the president.

Meanwhile the poet looks for solitude
beneath a mossy roof

a clutch of purple violets
or those trimmed in white.

It's raining
now the rain has stopped

steam rises from every cranny, crevice
to make a stream this stone can skip across.

ALTHOUGH IT WASN'T YOU

I thought I saw you in the street
just another curly haired woman

gone salt and pepper
of a certain age
walking with a certain stride

but it wasn't you
on the edge of Tuesday
on a run-down block
in a hot springs town

when we met
you were sleeping in your truck
and I remembered you
from another life

it's like seeing,
unexpectedly
a bank of red and golden tulips
beneath bare trees

or a little teahouse
tucked away
by a waterfall's
mossy stones

or like something
sad, a sign printed
with the names of women
killed by domestic violence

and their dates—
posted at eye level
next to traffic

for no obvious reason

or the ravaged face
of a stranger
looking 19th century
outside the closed bathhouse

or a novel by Kawabata
about a geisha and predictable
heartbreak
in snow country

that still
breaks my heart
as I turn page by page
reassured

that although you are not here
you know
where I am

and I believe you will come
if I call.

glows but once a year.
Paper lanterns hung
outside each small gingerbread Victorian,
candle flickering
in its silken or patterned paper,
round cocoon.

Holding your hand,
everything was lit up
from inside
like a far-flung sun.

NEBRASKA

I pay three dollars
to enter the dusty
overheated room
of the roadside museum

mammoth skeleton
rises huge as the moon
over the eroded striations
of badlands

like driving at night
with a stranger
who must tell the whole
sad story of her life

things are closer
than we realize
or further away

the gift shop
has split-your-own geodes
and a star map
tacked to the wall

driving through Harrison
I buy two potatoes
and an onion
for soup

from a woman
who doesn't ask how I am
just clutches a cigarette
steps out on to the porch to smoke.

A Blue Window

seen from mine
in the old hotel

slick streets beneath
a stuttering street lamp

it's been many years
since I looked out
at rooms above mine

that particular
feeling—a hot springs town
in rain

you gave me a gift
hidden within the ordinary

a cafe life
small waterfall
Lakota star quilt

hiding in plain sight
a flicker
of the ineffable

taste or scent
of spring in autumn

curtain pulled back
light spilling
out

Geology of the High Plains

something burrows
under the house

and two hawks flying parallel
dive towards
some other creature
in the field

a songbird hits the window

and I
make a cup of coffee

I'm worried
I've been unkind

a mask in the world
of forms
firelight flickering

this was once a shallow inland sea
(weren't we all…once)

schist and quartzite
gneissic visible layers

I've been unkind
and worse
I've failed to fight
on my own behalf

that's over now.

Spelunker

the girl vanishes
from the cave—
separated
from her partner,
she falls into a crevice
is rescued
thirty hours later

she's been singing—
when they find her
she is belting the last verse
of "All Along
the Watchtower"
for the hundredth or more time

not everyone
knows enough lyrics
to survive
solitary confinement
but I do—
for hours south on 71
South Dakota to Nebraska
I've been singing
"Boys and Girls Together"
and "The Cape Cod girls
they have no combs"

Besides the moon
that was the first thing
I ever noticed was beautiful,
these words:
"They comb their hair
with codfish bones"

I'm just in the cave
for an hour,
in total darkness
for the few minutes
the Park Service allows—
bauxite, calcite,
a crust
of sparkling crystals
and every song a song of the sea
that left so long ago.

RAPABLE...

I must be a woman

although the goddess Tara
attained enlightenment
she didn't change bodies

so I'm
two things at once

female form
empty

the bones of the Miocene
dance with stars
marking every
mammalian joint

if there is a mouse here
I haven't seen it yet

just a little girl
with pigtails
drawing on pavement

here at the end of an age
here at the end

Is EVERYTHING EVERYWHERE?

Once you know
for sure

please
tell me.

THE MOUNTAIN IS A WHETSTONE

it sharpens
the sickle of the moon

as war
sharpens hunger

and solitude–
compassion

in 144 hours
god created

earth, leviathan,
the days of the week

although
you and I

have been
parted

I know for sure
we'll meet again.

LIVING EACH DAY

as if it were my last
or at least
pretending to
I eat one
delicious
half of a macaroon
and then the other half

I'm not staying
alive
for any
particular reason—
not even for your love
or the fight
for justice
or the pleasure
of sliced cake
in a glass case
can keep my feet
forever on this earth.

I drink coffee
I don't know
what I'm doing
in the afternoon air
of Tuesday
like a red bird
on a leafless bough
of redbud.

BEASTS is set in Avenir Next, a late twentieth century font designed by Adrian Frutiger.